HANDBOOK OF C(
NEW ZEAL.
BIRDS

HANDBOOK OF COMMON NEW ZEALAND BIRDS

F.C. Kinsky and C.J.R. Robertson

Illustrations by Janet Marshall

REED

ACKNOWLEDGEMENTS

The artist and the authors wish to acknowledge the assistance and advice of G. Marshall, the National Museum and the staff of the New Zealand Wildlife Service.

Published by Reed Books, a division of Reed Publishing Group (NZ) Ltd, 39 Rawene Road, Birkenhead, Auckland. Associated companies, branches and representatives throughout the world.

This book is copyright. Except for the purpose of fair reviewing, no part of this publication may be reproduced or transmitted in any form or by any means, electronic or mechanical, including photocopying, recording, or any information storage and retrieval system, without permission in writing from the publisher. Infringers of copyright render themselves liable to prosecution.

ISBN 0 7900 0145 4

© 1987 F.C Kinsky and C.J.R. Robertson (text)
         J. Marshall (paintings)

First published 1987
Reprinted 1989, 1991, 1993, 1994

Designed by Karol Wilczynski
Typset be Filmset Type Ltd Auckland
Printed in Singapore

Contents

	Page	Plate
Introduction	1	
Notes on Text	3	
Brown Kiwi	5	1
Yellow-eyed Penguin	7	2
Fiordland Crested Penguin	7	2
Blue Penguin	9	3
White-flippered Penguin	9	3
New Zealand Dabchick	11	4
Australasian Gannet	13	5
Black Shag	15	6
Pied Shag	15	6
Little Black Shag	17	7
Little Shag	17	7
Stewart Island Shag	19	8
Spotted Shag	21	9
White-faced Heron	23	10
White Heron	25	11
Royal Spoonbill	25	11
Reef Heron	27	12
Bittern	29	13
Black Swan	31	14
Mute Swan	31	
Canada Goose	33	15
Paradise Shelduck	35	16
Mallard	37	17
Grey Duck	39	18
New Zealand Scaup	41	19
Grey Teal	41	19
New Zealand Shoveler	43	20
Blue Duck	45	21
Australasian Harrier	47	22

	Page	Plate
New Zealand Falcon	49	23
California Quail	51	24
Brown Quail	51	
Pheasant	53	25
Banded Rail	55	26
Weka	57	27
Pukeko	59	28
Australasian Coot	61	29
South Island Pied Oystercatcher	63	30
Variable Oystercatcher	63	30
Spur-winged Plover	65	31
Banded Dotterel	67	32
Black-fronted Dotterel	69	33
Wrybill	71	34
Eastern Bar-tailed Godwit	73	35
Pied Stilt	75	36
Southern Black-backed Gull	77	37
Red-billed Gull	79	38
Black-billed Gull	81	39
Black-fronted Tern	83	40
Caspian Tern	85	41
White-fronted Tern	87	42
New Zealand Pigeon	89	43
Rock Pigeon	91	44
Kaka	93	45
Kea	93	45
Eastern Rosella	95	46
Red-crowned Parakeet	97	47
Yellow-crowned Parakeet	97	47
Shining Cuckoo	99	48
Long-tailed Cuckoo	99	48
Morepork	101	49
Little Owl	103	50

	Page	Plate
Kingfisher	105	51
Rifleman	107	52
Rock Wren	109	53
Skylark	111	54
New Zealand Pipit	111	54
Welcome Swallow	113	55
Hedge Sparrow	115	56
Fernbird	117	57
Brown Creeper	119	58
Whitehead	121	59
Yellowhead	123	60
Grey Warbler	125	61
Fantail	127	62
Tit	129	63
Robin	131	64
Song Thrush	133	65
Blackbird	135	66
Silvereye	137	67
Bellbird	139	68
Tui	141	69
Yellowhammer	143	70
Cirl Bunting	143	70
Chaffinch	145	71
Greenfinch	147	72
Goldfinch	149	73
Redpoll	151	74
House Sparrow	153	75
Starling	155	76
Indian Myna	157	77
Black-backed Magpie	159	78
White-backed Magpie	161	79
Rook	163	80
Index of Common Names	164	

Introduction

There has been an increasing number of books devoted to New Zealand birds in recent years. However, the tendency has been to write about, photograph and paint only the native or endemic species and to ignore the numerous introduced birds which have become an integral part of the New Zealand bird fauna.

This book focuses on those birds, both native and introduced, which are most frequently seen. It is not designed as a field guide or a text book, but for use in practical visual identification. The colour portraits, which present a clear image for each species, are complemented by a brief summary of information about the bird. The object of the book is to give the reader an incentive for further study rather than to provide an exhaustive reference, which may well prove to be too detailed for those with only a general interest in birds.

Few people are unaware of the birds inhabiting our environment. Many of the most commonly seen birds have been introduced since 1850. Some of these have replaced those native and endemic species which have failed to survive our modification of the environment and the preying of introduced animals, such as cats and rats.

Some birds, both native and introduced, are considered pests because they compete with humans for the produce of crops, orchards and even the vegetable garden, which provide an abundant and varied food store. The resulting losses are invariably followed by demands for control and even extermination. Unfortunately, the end result is often the destruction of species other than the ones we are trying to destroy. Many birds, including those often considered troublesome, perform a useful function in controlling naturally other animal pests without the cost of chemicals and the increasing side-effects of pollution.

The rapid modification of the land for towns, industry and agriculture has resulted in the loss of valuable forest and wetland habitat which has seriously affected many species. Regrettably, decisions pertaining to reservations of original bush more often relate to economics than the ecological requirments of birds and trees.

Unfortunately, the true numbers and habits of many of our native birds are relatively unknown. The result is that public debate on conservation issues is based more often on emotion rather than fact. In many cases, the birds which are used as arguments to preserve an area have been so affected by other factors that the preservation or removal of the bush or wetland will have little effect on them.

However, the growing interest in conservation and the demand for more knowledge about changes in the environment are encouraging. Interest and knowledge are the first steps towards the action which is required to prevent the endangering of further bird species in the future. We hope that this book will stimulate your interest, both at home and while travelling, and improve your understanding. All birds have their place and importance. Let us conserve and enjoy what we have, regardless of sentiment and without differentiation.

Notes on Text

The birds appear in the same order as in the **Annotated Checklist of the Birds of New Zealand** except where two species are shown on one plate. Common, scientific and, where available, Maori names are shown according to the **Checklist**.

Species are divided into four categories:

Endemic — confined solely to the New Zealand region.

Native — naturally occurring in New Zealand, but also found elsewhere in the world.

Introduced — introduced by human agency.

Migrant — breeding overseas, but regularly visiting New Zealand for part of the non-breeding season.

Scientific names are the only certain way of referring to any bird, as common names so often vary throughout the country and may be shared by several species.

Though we have tried to use simple language for all descriptions, an occasional specific term has been used.

Male — ♂   Female — ♀

BROWN KIWI

Plate 1

Brown Kiwi
(Kiwi)

Apteryx australis
Family: APTERYGIDAE

Endemic: Three sub-species. North Island (shown in plate), South Island and Stewart Island. (Fully protected.)

Field Characters:
— size of large domestic fowl.
— loose, coarse bristly feathers.
— long thin bill with nostrils at tip.
— flightless, remnants of wings concealed in plumage.
— moves about only at night, hidden in burrows during day.
— Voice: an often repeated shrill whistle "ki-weee" in male, hoarse and lower pitched in female.
— *North Island:* darkest and smallest, dark legs.
— *South Island:* lighter and softer plumage, pale flesh-coloured legs.
— *Stewart Island:* similar to South Island but with dark legs. (Largest of group).

Distribution and Habitat:
— throughout New Zealand in native bush, second growth and scrubland.
— least common in South Island, mainly found in Fiordland and South Westland.
— feeds on worms, insects, berries and seeds, most located by smell.

Breeding:
— throughout year especially July to February.
— Nest: in hollow logs, under tree roots, and in holes in banks.
— Eggs: normally 1-2, smooth ivory or greenish-white.
— male only incubates and cares for young.

Note:
   The Little Spotted Kiwi *(Apteryx oweni)* and Great Spotted Kiwi *Apteryx haasti)* are found in the South Island generally west of the main divide. Coloured grey, banded and mottled with brownish-black. These are respectively the smallest and largest of the Kiwis.

Yellow-eyed Penguin
(Hoiho)

Megadyptes antipodes
Family: SPHENISCIDAE

Endemic: (Fully Protected.)

Field Characters:
— largest of New Zealand mainland penguins.
— Adult: distinctive yellow eye and yellow band right round head.
— Immature: grey eye and no yellow band.

Distribution and Habitat:
— on coast from Banks Peninsula to Southland and Stewart Island, straggling to Cook Strait.
— feeds on small fish and squid.

Breeding:
— September to December.
— Nest: of sticks and coarse grass in scattered colonies throughout scrubland or coastal bush, sometimes up to 100 m.
— Eggs: 2, white.

Fiordland Crested Penguin (Tawaki)

Eudyptes pachyrhynchus
Family: SPHENISCIDAE

Endemic: (Fully protected.)

Field Characters:
— strongly hooked heavy bill.
— yellow stripe above eye extending backwards into separate crests.
— white bases to cheek feathers obvious when bird is excited.
— Immature: white throat, little or no crest.

Distribution and Habitat:
— South Westland, Fiordland and Stewart Island in coastal native bush.
— feeds on small fish, squid and krill.

Breeding:
— July to September.
— Nest: of sticks and leaves in scattered colonies among rocks, in caves and cavities beneath tree roots.
— Eggs: 1-2, white.

Note: Other species of crested Penguins breed on New Zealand sub-antarctic islands and straggle to the mainland.

Blue Penguin
(Korora)

Eudyptula minor
Family: SPHENISCIDAE

Plate 3

Native: Several closely related sub-species in New Zealand. Also occurs in Southern Australia from Perth to Sydney and Tasmania. (Fully protected.)

Field Characters:
— smallest of all penguins.
— variable shades of blue on back, white below.
— nocturnal on land and except when breeding spends day at sea.
— males have heavier bills than females.
— long wailing call of variable pitch.

Distribution and Habitat:
— plentiful round New Zealand coasts.
— feeds mainly on small fish and fish larvae.

Breeding:
— August to November.
— Nest: of grasses and sticks in caves, crevices, under boulders, in self-dug burrows under stumps, small bushes and flax up to 350 m.
— Sometimes under houses and in sheds.
— Eggs: 1-2, white.

White-flippered Penguin

Eudyptula albosignata
Family: SPHENISCIDAE

Plate 3

Endemic: Can be considered a sub-species of Blue Penguin. (Fully protected.)

Field Characters:
— larger and lighter in colour than Blue Penguin.
— front edge of flipper white.
— variable amount of white on tail and rump.

Distribution and Habitat:
— generally Banks Peninsula and Canterbury coast where it is locally plentiful.
— straggling to Cook Strait in North and Otago Peninsula in South.
— habitat and food as for Blue Penguin.

Breeding:
— August to November.
— Nest and Eggs: similar to Blue Penguin.

New Zealand Dabchick
(Weweia)

Podiceps rufopectus
Family: PODICIPEDIDAE

Plate 4

Endemic: (Fully protected.)

Field Characters:
— half-size of Grey Duck.
— small head, short pointed bill.
— throat and upper chest reddish-brown.
— underparts white with brown mottling on flanks.
— no tail, rump high when swimming.
— rapid head-first dive.
— Immature: cheeks grey, throat and upper chest pale reddish-brown, underparts white.

Distribution and Habitat:
— North Island lakes, ponds, and coastal lagoons, rare in South Island.
— not generally on rivers.
— feeds in shallow fresh water on insects and snails.

Breeding:
— August to May.
— Nest: flimsy but bulky structure floating among and attached to water-edge vegetation.
— Eggs: 2-3, chalky-white quickly stained yellowish-brown, covered with weed when unattended.
— small chicks with striped plumage may be carried on the backs of swimming parents.

Australasian Gannet
(Takapu)

Sula bassana
Family: SULIDAE

Plate 5

Native: Also occurs Southern Australia. Two related sub-species in South Africa and North Atlantic. (Fully protected.)

Field Characters:
— the size of a goose.
— Adult: white body contrasting with black trailing edge of wing. Yellow head not obvious at sea.
— Juvenile: white undersides, grey streaked head and neck, slate-grey back with white spots.
— often in flocks, diving from considerable height for food.

Distribution and Habitat:
— mainly round North Island in summer, dispersing widely in winter.
— breeding mainly on offshore islands round northern half of North Island.
— only mainland colonies at Cape Kidnappers and Muriwai.
— most juveniles spend at least first two years in Australian waters.
— feeds by diving for small fish and squid.

Breeding:
— August to December.
— Nest: cup-shaped mound of seaweed, grasses and iceplant cemented with droppings, in closely packed colonies.
— Eggs: 1, pale bluish or greenish-white with chalky surface.

Black Shag
(Kawau)

Plate 6

Phalacrocorax carbo
Family: PHALACROCORACIDAE

Native: Similar sub-species also in Australia, Europe, Africa, Asia and North America. (Partially protected.)

Field Characters:
— largest shag in New Zealand.
— white thigh patch, and greenish-black head plumes only in breeding season.
— Immature: browner than adult, and generally lighter on undersides.

Distribution and Habitat:
— throughout country on inland lakes, rivers, lagoons and sea coast.
— feeds by diving from surface for fish, freshwater crayfish and eels.
— there is little factual evidence to support reputed damage to trout fisheries.

Breeding:
— April to May and September to October, possibly 2 broods.
— Nest: large, of sticks, in colonies either on high trees or rock ledges, and on lower vantage points, close to, or surrounded by water.
— Eggs: 3-4, pale bluish-green with white chalky outer layer.

Pied Shag
(Kahuriruhi)

Plate 6

Phalacrocorax varius
Family: PHALACROCORACIDAE

Native: Similar sub-species also in Australia. (Fully protected.)

Field Characters:
— slightly smaller than Black Shag.
— sides of face, neck, underparts white, thighs black.
— Immature: blackish-brown above, white below variably mottled with blackish-brown.

Distribution and Habitat:
— on coast throughout country, more numerous in north of both main islands, and Stewart Island, rarely inland.
— feeds mainly on marine fish, and occasionally in freshwater.

Breeding:
— Similar to Black Shag, often in mixed colonies with Black Shags, and Little Shags.
— Eggs: 2-4, pale blue, covered with white chalky outer layer.

Little Black Shag *Phalacrocorax sulcirostris*
Family: PHALACROCORACIDAE

Plate 7

Native: Also Australia and South-west Pacific. (Fully Protected.)

Field Characters:
— slightly smaller than Little Shag.
— long slender *dark* bill and *short* tail.
— no crest at any stage.
— scalloped appearance of back and wing plumage.

Distribution and Habitat:
— North Island, more common in northern half, breeding in only a few localities.
— fresh-water lakes, salt-water lagoons and coast.
— feeds often in groups, by diving from surface, on small fish and eels.

Breeding:
— possibly February to May, September to December.
— Nest: of sticks and grasses in tree colonies, may be mixed with colonies of Little Shags, Black and Pied Shags.
— Eggs; 2-4, pale blue with white chalky outer layer.

Little Shag (Kawaupaka) *Phalacrocorax melanoleucos*
Family: PHALACROCORACIDAE

Plate 7

Native: Similar sub-species in Australia and South-west Pacific. (Fully protected.)

Field Characters:
— small shag.
— short *yellow* bill, *long* tail.
— Adult: white cheeks and variable amount of white on undersides from white throat only to completely white below. Small black crest on forehead in breeding season.
— Immature: *All* black with *yellow* bill.

Distribution and Habitat:
— throughout country on fresh water, coastline, and into mountains.
— most common of freshwater shags.
— feeds by diving from surface on fish, eels, fresh water crayfish and aquatic insect larvae.

(Continued on page 19)

Plate 8

Stewart Island Shag

Leucocarbo carunculatus chalconotus
Family: **PHALACROCORACIDAE**

Endemic: Two closely related sub-species in New Zealand. (Fully protected.)

Field Characters:
— slightly smaller than Black Shag.
— two colour phases *"Bronze"* and *"Pied"* in approximately equal proportions.
— conspicuous white wing and back patches distinguish "Pied Phase" from Pied Shag in Plate 6.
— *pink* feet.
— large head prominent in flight.

Distribution and Habitat:
— from Otago Peninsula to Foveaux Strait and Stewart Island.
— only in coastal waters.
— feeds on small fish.

Breeding:
— July to September.
— Nest: cup-shaped of grasses and seaweed cemented with droppings, in tight colonies on cliffs and rocky islands.
— Eggs: 2-3, pale green with thin white chalky outer layer.
— both "phases" interbreed producing either "bronze" or "pied" young.

(Continued from page 17)
Breeding:
— September to November.
— Nest: of sticks in colonies above or near water, often mixed with Pied and Black Shags.
— Eggs: 3-4, pale blue with white chalky outer layer.

Spotted Shag
(Parekareka)

Stictocarbo punctatus
Family: **PHALACROCORACIDAE**

Plate 9

Endemic: Two closely related sub-species in New Zealand. (Fully protected.)

Field Characters:
— large slender shag.
— generally dark grey above and light grey below with white stripe along side of head and neck.
— feet, variably pale whitish-yellow to chrome-yellow.
— Adult: shows ornamental crest and plumes *only* during early breeding season.
— Immature: all grey head and underparts.

Distribution and Habitat:
— common, but patchily distributed throughout North and South Island.
— only seen on coast.
— feeds on small fish and crustacea.

Breeding:
— Throughout year.
— Nest: of sticks, cliff plants and seaweed, in colonies on ledges, fissures in steep cliffs or sea caves preferably with overhead cover.
— Eggs: 2-4, pale blue with chalky outer layer.

Note: Blue Shag *(Stictocarbo p. steadi)* generally found at Stewart Island, Foveaux Strait, and West Coast of South Island. Somewhat darker in plumage.

WHITE – FACED HERON

White-faced Heron

Ardea novaehollandiae
Family: ARDEIDAE

Plate 10

Native: Self-introduced from Australia, rare till 1940s. (Fully protected.)

Field Characters:
— white face, light blue-grey body.
— dark grey wing feathers contrasting in flight with paler body.
— neck retracted in flight.
— slow, leisurely wing beat.
— Immature: generally similar to adult, but with indistinct white face.

Distribution and Habitat:
— most common heron, widespread throughout New Zealand.
— all habitats except bush, rarely alpine, usually seashore, ponds, lakes, rivers, and open pasture.
— often perches on trees and fence posts.
— may be seen in large groups.
— feeds mainly on land and water insects (dragonflies, grasshoppers, blowflies, etc.), also fish, frogs and small mammals.

Breeding:
— August to December.
— Nest: small, untidy, flimsy, of sticks, found singly in high trees. (Not colonial.)
— Eggs: 3-5, light blue with white chalky marks.

White Heron
(Kotuku)

Egretta alba
Family: ARDEIDAE

Native: Also Australia and closely related sub-species throughout world. (Fully protected.)

Field Characters:
— larger than Reef Heron.
— Pure white, *yellow* bill, black legs.
— adult bill black *only* during early breeding season.
— neck retracted in flight, slow leisurely wing beat.

Distribution and Habitat:
— in small numbers throughout country, breeding *only* at Okarito, South Westland.
— disperse outside breeding season generally to lake edges, ponds and marshes.
— feeds on small fish, frogs, insects and occasionally small birds with quick stabbing of bill.

Breeding:
— September to October.
— Nest: of twigs in colony on low trees and tree ferns near water.
— Eggs: 3-4, pale bluish-green.

Royal Spoonbill
(Kotuku-ngutu-papa)

Platalea regia
Family: THRESKIORNITHIDAE

Native: Self-introduced since 1850s, also in Australia and New Guinea. (Fully protected.)

Field Characters:
— slightly bigger than White Heron.
— face, large flattened bill and legs black.
— neck, *extended* in flight.
— Immature; varying amount of black on flight feathers visible when flying.

Distribution and Habitat:
— less common than White Heron, throughout country, has only bred at Okarito and Wairau Lagoon.
— disperses to river estuaries and lagoons outside breeding season.
— feeds on small crustacea in *shallow* water by sidesweeping tip of bill through water.

(Continued on page 27)

REEF HERON

Reef Heron
(Matuku-moana)

Egretta sacra
Family: ARDEIDAE

Plate 12

Native: Also Asia, Australia and South-west Pacific. (Fully protected.)
Note: A white form occurs throughout northern part of range outside New Zealand.

Field Characters:
— Similar to, but *much darker* than White-faced Heron.
— dark slate-blue all over.
— neck retracted in flight, slow leisurely wing beat.
— normally singly or in pairs.

Distribution and Habitat:
— throughout country only on sheltered rocky coastline, becoming more sparingly distributed.
— commonest in northern half of North Island and larger offshore islands, frequenting mudflats and intertidal zone.
— feeds close inshore on small fish and crabs.

Breeding:
— September to February.
— Nest: of sticks, well hidden in shallow caves or crevices, or among bushes on steep cliffs, not far from water.
— Eggs: usually 3, pale greenish-blue.

(Continued from page 25)
Breeding:
— November to December
— Nest: of sticks, in colony.
— Eggs: 3-4, white, sparingly marked with brown blotches.

Bittern
(Matuku)

Botaurus stellaris
Family: ARDEIDAE

Plate 13

Native: Also found Australia and New Caledonia.
(Fully protected.)

Field Characters:
— bulkier than White-faced Heron with shorter legs, and neck appearing stout and shorter.
— all buff-brown with dark streaking.
— in flight, slow wing beat, with neck tucked in.
— if disturbed in cover often "freezes" with head and bill erect.
— very secretive.
— Voice: loud booming at night.

Distribution and Habitat:
— throughout New Zealand, rarely seen in open.
— swamps, lakes, salt marshes and boggy areas with cover.
— feeds on wide variety of food, mainly insects, fish and eels, frogs and small mammals.

Breeding:
— September to January.
— Nest: large firm platform of rushes, reeds and sticks, usually surrounded by water and well hidden in reed beds and between clumps of niggerheads.
— Eggs: 4-5, plain brownish-cream, without spots.

BLACK SWAN

Plate 14

Black Swan *Cygnus atratus*
Family: ANATIDAE

Introduced: From Australia prior to 1864 and during 1860s in both islands. (Protected but may be hunted in open season in some localities.)

Field Characters:
— very large, predominantly black.
— white wing feathers conspicuous in flight.
— bill mainly ruby-red.
— outstretched neck in flight, ponderous wing beat.
— Immature: grey, with dark bill.

Distribution and Habitat:
— throughout New Zealand on medium to large lakes and lagoons.
— mainly coastal, rare in some districts, but large breeding populations, especially at Lake Ellesmere and the Waikato lakes.
— feeds on water plants in shallow water to greater depth than ducks.

Breeding:
— Mainly August to November.
— Nest: substantial mound of grass and rushes lined with down and close to water, normally single surrounded by tall vegetation. By some large lakes (e.g. Lake Ellesmere) colonial breeding on open ground.
— Eggs: 4-7, greenish-white.

Mute Swan *Cygnus olor*

Note: A rare, larger, pure white swan, with orange bill and prominent black knob at base of bill, may be seen occasionally associated with flocks of Black Swan in the wild (fully protected). Introduced originally for ornamental purposes and still seen in public parks.

CANADA GOOSE

Canada Goose

Branta canadensis
Family: ANATIDAE

Plate 15

Introduced: From North America 1876-1905. (Not protected, except in certain areas.)

Field Characters:
— somewhat smaller than Black Swan, with shorter neck.
— colour buff, with black neck and white cheeks.
— in flight, outstretched neck, fast wingbeat.
— Immature: black parts are dark brown.

Distribution and Habitat:
— South Island, east of main divide, rare in North Island, except at Tauranga Harbour and northern Hawke's Bay.
— high country and larger lakes where they may concentrate in large moulting flocks during late summer.
— feeds on grass and green fodder crops.

Breeding:
— October to December.
— Nest: on ground, of grasses and tussock lined with down, generally in high country.
— Eggs: 4-7, creamy-white.
— Female only incubates, male usually on guard nearby.

PARADISE SHELDUCK ♀

♂

Paradise Shelduck
(Putangitangi)

Tadorna variegata
Family: ANATIDAE

Plate 16

Endemic: (Protected but may be hunted in open season in some localities.)

Field Characters:
— size between Mallard and Canada Goose.
— Male: predominantly black with metallic sheen on head.
— Female: white head, dark back, rusty brown undersides.
— in flight, both sexes show prominent large white patch on wing.
— Immature: similar to adult male.

Distribution and Habitat:
— throughout both islands reaching high density in some areas, generally increasing where protected.
— open hill country, riverbeds, small lakes and ponds, and open pasture.
— large moulting flocks on some lakes in late summer.
— feeds on soft grasses and herbs, some insects.

Breeding:
— August to January.
— Nest: of grass and down, generally well hidden on ground, sometimes in hollow trees up to 6 m.
— not necessarily adjacent to water.
— Eggs: 5-11, cream.
— female only incubates, but male assists in rearing young.

MALLARD DUCK

♀

♂

Mallard

Anas platyrynchos
Family: ANATIDAE

Plate 17

Introduced: From Britain since 1867 and later also from USA. Extensive liberations from hand-reared stock till 1950s. (Protected but may be hunted in open season.)

Field Characters:
— Male: two plumages, "breeding plumage", very conspicuous as in plate.
— "Eclipse plumage" (late summer and autumn) similar to female, but male recognisable by *olive-green* bill.
— Female: may be confused with Grey Duck, but is a browner bird generally lacking striped face.
— orange feet, bill *dark olive-brown* with individually variable orange mottling.
— speculum (patch on wing) shiny blue, with white stripe at both margins.
— pale sides to tail showing in flight.
— Immature: like female.

Distribution and Habitat:
— throughout New Zealand
— rapidly increasing in proportion to Grey Duck, especially in south.
— habitat and feeding as for Grey Duck.

Breeding:
— August to December.
— Nest: similar to Grey Duck but often close to water or margins of wetlands in any available cover (e.g., niggerheads and in raupo).
— Eggs: 5-20, cream with light green tinge.
— female only incubates and cares for young.

Note: Extensive interbreeding with ducks of similar size (including domestic) has produced widely mixed hybrid plumages.

GREY DUCK

Grey Duck
(Parera)

Anas superciliosa
Family: ANATIDAE

Plate 18

Native: Also Australia. (Protected but may be hunted in open season.)

Field Characters:
— somewhat smaller than Mallard.
— male and female indistinguishable.
— conspicuous black stripe from bill through eye, otherwise face and chin light buff.
— speculum glossy green with inconspicuous white stripe *only* on lower margin.
— feet yellowish-brown.
— bill uniformly dark greyish-blue.

Distribution and Habitat:
— throughout New Zealand more plentiful in north.
— rivers, lakes, ponds, swamps and inter-tidal mudflats.
— feeds on plants or small insects either on land or in shallow water.
— in shallow water, dabbling or "up-ending" is typical.

Breeding:
— September to December.
— Nest: dry grass and other vegetation, lined with down, generally away from water, well hidden under cover, on the ground, but occasionally in hollow trees or tree forks.
— Eggs: 5-11, greenish-cream.
— female only incubates and cares for young.

Note: Extensive interbreeding with the Mallard has produced hybrids which may show characteristics of both species.

NEW ZEALAND SCAUP ♀

GREY TEAL

New Zealand Scaup
(Papango)

Aythya novaeseelandiae
Family: ANATIDAE

Plate 19

Endemic: (Fully protected.)

Field Characters:
— all dark, plump, small duck.
— Male: striking yellow eye and dark head.
— Female: white face patch in breeding plumage, dark eye.
— conspicuous white wing bar on both sexes in flight.
— dives deep for food.

Distribution and Habitat:
— localised throughout both islands on freshwater lakes and ponds.

Breeding:
— October to March.
— Nest: of grass lined with down, close to water, in dense cover or under banks. Often in close groups.
— Eggs: 5-8, creamy-white.

Grey Teal
(Tete)

Anas gibberifrons
Family: ANATIDAE

Plate 19

Native: Also Australia. (Fully protected.)

Field Characters:
— much smaller than Grey Duck, but often mistakenly shot as such. Sexes alike.
— rapid wing beat, often seen in wheeling flocks.
— speculum (patch on wing) greenish-black, with broad white bar on upper and narrow white bar on lower margin.
— in flight a prominent white triangle shows on underwing with its base close to body.

Distribution and Habitat:
— throughout both islands, more plentiful since 1950s, highly mobile.
— lakes, ponds, lagoons.
— feeds by dabbling, on water insects, snails and plants.

(Continued on page 43)

NEW ZEALAND SHOVELER

New Zealand Shoveler
(Kuruwhengi)

Anas rhynchotis
Family: ANATIDAE

Plate 20

Endemic: Closely related race in Australia. (Protected, but may be hunted in open season.)

Field Characters:
— smaller than Mallard.
— prominent wide bill pointed downwards when swimming.
— Male: "breeding plumage", striking white facial crescent, prominent white patch on flank (lightness of upper breast is variable). "Eclipse plumage" similar to female.
— Female: colouring like female Mallard but with striking powder-blue patch on upper wing.

Distribution and Habitat:
— throughout New Zealand, plentiful in some areas, highly mobile.
— lakes, lagoons, mainly near coast.
— feeds by dabbling.

Breeding:
— October to January.
— Nest: near water (often along ditches), generally of grasses lined with down, among long grass in open areas.
— Eggs: 10-13, pale creamy-white.
— female only incubates, but male assists in rearing young.

(Continued from page 41)
Breeding:
— September to January.
— Nest: of grass, generally lined with down, under vegetation, near water, or in trees.
— Eggs: 5-9, dark-cream.

BLUE DUCK

Blue Duck
(Whio)

Hymenolaimus malacoryhynchos
Family: ANATIDAE

Plate 21

Endemic: (Fully protected.)

Field Characters:
— smaller than Mallard.
— dove grey, heavily spotted with chestnut on breast.
— prominent narrow bill, pinkish-white with black edge to tip.
— Immature: similar, but no chestnut spotting on breast.
— Male has characteristic whistling call; females a gutteral rattle.
— singly, in pairs or family groups.

Distribution and Habitat:
— North and South Islands now restricted to fast-flowing mountain and bush streams in undeveloped areas.
— feeds by diving mainly for insect larvae.

Breeding:
— August to November.
— Nest: lined with down, on ground under thick vegetation or in holes, close to or above a stream.
— Eggs: 4-9, creamy-white.

AUSTRALASIAN HARRIER

Immature

Adult

Australasian Harrier
(Kahu)

Circus approximans
Family: ACCIPITRIDAE

Plate 22

Native: Also in Australia and S.W. Pacific (Partially protected.)

Field Characters:
— large bird of prey.
— adults, in contrast to chocolate-brown immature birds, have light buff undersides, with dark streaking.
— some old males appear almost white, with silvery-grey wings.
— in flight, often soars with wings tipped upwards giving broad "vee" image.

Distribution and Habitat:
— fairly common throughout New Zealand except in heavily-forested districts and alpine areas.
— diminishing in numbers by removal of the rabbit and through persecution.
— generally seen singly or in pairs, out of breeding season occasionally flocking at night roosts in swamps.
— feeds mainly on small mammals, insects, lizards, carrion and occasionally small birds, often seen eating road killed animals.

Breeding:
— October to December.
— Nest: platform of tussock and small sticks on ground, mostly in swamps and scrub areas.
— Eggs, commonly 4, chalky-white.

NEW ZEALAND FALCON

Adult ♀

Immature ♂

New Zealand Falcon
(Karearea)

Falco novaeseelandiae
Family: FALCONIDAE

Plate 23

Endemic: (Fully protected.)

Field Characters:
— about half size of Australian Harrier.
— Females generally much larger than males.
— Adult: upper parts appearing black, but feathers striped with buff.
— underparts light cream with dark streaks, thighs rusty red.
— feet and naked skin at base of bill, yellow.
— Immature: dark blackish-brown above and all dark chocolate-brown below.
— feet and naked skin at base of bill, lead-grey.
— call a piercing whistle or scream, "kek kek kek".

Distribution and Habitat:
— distributed generally throughout New Zealand in native bush and isolated high back-country valleys.
— feeds mainly on birds up to duck size and occasionally small mammals, reptiles and larger insects.

Breeding:
— October to November.
— Nest: scrape of grass or sticks under overhanging rocks on steep slopes or in high trees.
— Eggs: 2-4, rich reddish-brown with darker blotches.
— female only incubates.

CALIFORNIA QUAIL

♂

♀

California Quail *Lophortyx californius*
Family: PHASIANIDAE

Plate 24

Introduced: From USA 1862. (Protected, but may be hunted in open season in some localities.)

Field Characters:
— black crest larger in male than female.
— male's black face surrounded by white band.
— when disturbed rises with a loud "whirring".
— often perches on trees and fence posts.

Distribution and Habitat:
— throughout New Zealand, plentiful in some areas (e.g., Taupo, Marlborough, Central Otago).
— generally farmland with hedges and scrub, occasionally in gardens.
— outside breeding season, mainly in coveys or family groups.
— feeds mainly on seeds and soft grasses.

Breeding:
— October to December.
— simple grass nest in ground hollow near or under cover.
— Eggs: 9-16, creamy-yellow blotched all over with dark brown.
— females only incubate.

Brown Quail *Synoicus ypsilophorus*

Note: Introduced from Australia, confined to North Island and numerous in Auckland district. Smaller than Californian, all brown, no crest.

PHEASANT

Pheasant

Phasianus colchicus
Family: PHASIANIDAE

Plate 25

Introduced: Of mixed origins since 1842. Wild stock still supplemented by annual liberations. (Protected but may be hunted in open season.)

Field Characters:
— Male: colourful, but varied through hybridisation, some having white neck ring.
— long barred tail.
— Female: drab and slightly smaller.

Distribution and Habitat:
— patchy wild distribution mainly in North Island and eastern coastal areas of South Island.
— scrublands and hedgerows.
— feeds on berries, seeds and insects.

Breeding:
— September to January.
— Nest: scantily-lined hollow in thick cover.
— Eggs: 6-14, uniform olive-brown.
— female only incubates and cares for young.
— one cock often breeds with more than one female.

BANDED RAIL

Banded Rail
(Moho-pereru)

Rallus phillippensis
Family: RALLIDAE

Plate 26

Native: Also related sub-species in S.E. Asia, Australia and S.W. Pacific. (Fully protected.)

Field Characters:
— black and white striped pattern on underside.
— pronounced chestnut eye streak forming collar at the back of head.
— runs swiftly, rarely seen flying.
— very secretive.

Distribution and Habitat:
— throughout New Zealand, although common, is rarely seen.
— swamps, salt marsh lagoons, lake edges, mangroves, drainage ditches with cover.
— feeds on insects, worms, snails, seeds.

Breeding:
— September to February.
— Nest: of grasses or rushes, well hidden near or above water.
— Eggs: 4-7, pale pinkish-buff with scattered reddish-brown and purplish-grey spots and blotches.

WEKA

Western

North Island

Weka

Gallirallus australis
Family: RALLIDAE

Plate 27

Endemic: Four closely related sub-species, North Island and Western Weka shown in plate. (Fully protected except on Chatham Islands.)

Field Characters:
— inquisitive, flightless, measured walk, flicking tail, rapid run.
— *North Island:* smallest, with grey undersides and brown legs.
— *Western:* generally larger than North Island and with two colour phases, "Brown" phase similar to North Island, but with pink feet and less grey on underside. "Black" phase blackish-brown all over with red-brown feet.
— *Buff:* very similar to Western with red-brown legs and feet, also lighter (buff) plumage.
— *Stewart Island:* similar but smaller than Western with no dark streaking on flanks.

Distribution and Habitat:
— In North Island, restricted to Gisborne, Poverty Bay, but have recently been reintroduced to Northland and elsewhere.
— In South Island, Western Weka are locally common from Nelson-Marlborough to Fiordland generally west of main divide.
— Buff Weka previously on Canterbury Plains but restricted now to Chatham Islands (Introduced).
— Stewart Island Weka now present on Stewart Island and various southern islands where they were introduced by fishermen, whalers, sealers and mutton-birders.
— feeds on a wide variety of animal and vegetable matter, insects, crustacea, worms, fruits, rats and mice, eggs and chicks of ground-nesting birds.

Breeding:
— commonly September to April, but sometimes 3-4 times a year.
— Nest: shallow cup of woven grass under scrub, tussock, raupo according to locality.
— Eggs: 3-6, creamy-pink with scattered mauve blotches.

PUKEKO

Pukeko

Porphyrio porphyrio
Family: RALLIDAE

Plate 28

Native: Also in Australia. (Protected, but may be hunted in open season in some areas.)

Field Characters:
— bright blue and black.
— red bill, frontal shield and legs.
— often flicks tail to show prominent white under tail coverts.
— runs fast, is a reluctant flier, flying heavily with dangling legs.

Distribution and Habitat:
— throughout New Zealand.
— marshes, swamps, lagoons, lakes, riverbanks, with raupo and scrub cover.
— often seen in open near wetlands.
— feeds on wide variety of plant matter, snails, insects, sometimes eggs of other ground-nesting birds.

Breeding:
— August to March.
— Nest: bulky structure in swamp vegetation.
— Eggs: 4-8 normally reddish-cream with variable red-brown spots and purple blotches all over.

AUSTRALASIAN COOT

Australasian Coot

Fulica atra
Family: RALLIDAE

Plate 29

Native: Straggling from Australia since 1875, large increase and subsequent breeding in 1950s. (Fully protected.)

Field Characters:
— slightly smaller than Pukeko.
— mainly seen on water.
— all black with contrasting white bill and frontal shield.
— jerking head when swimming, dives frequently for food.
— Immature: grey with dark bill.

Distribution and Habitat:
— scattered pockets throughout both islands and increasing.
— breeding Otago, Canterbury, Wairarapa, Wanganui, Hawke's Bay, Rotorua and Auckland.
— frequents reed-fringed lakes.
— feeds on water plants, snails and insects.

Breeding:
— October to December.
— Nest: large and well hidden in swamp vegetation, of sticks and dead rushes according to habitat and neatly lined with raupo leaves.
— Eggs: 5-7, brownish-cream minutely dotted with black spots all over.

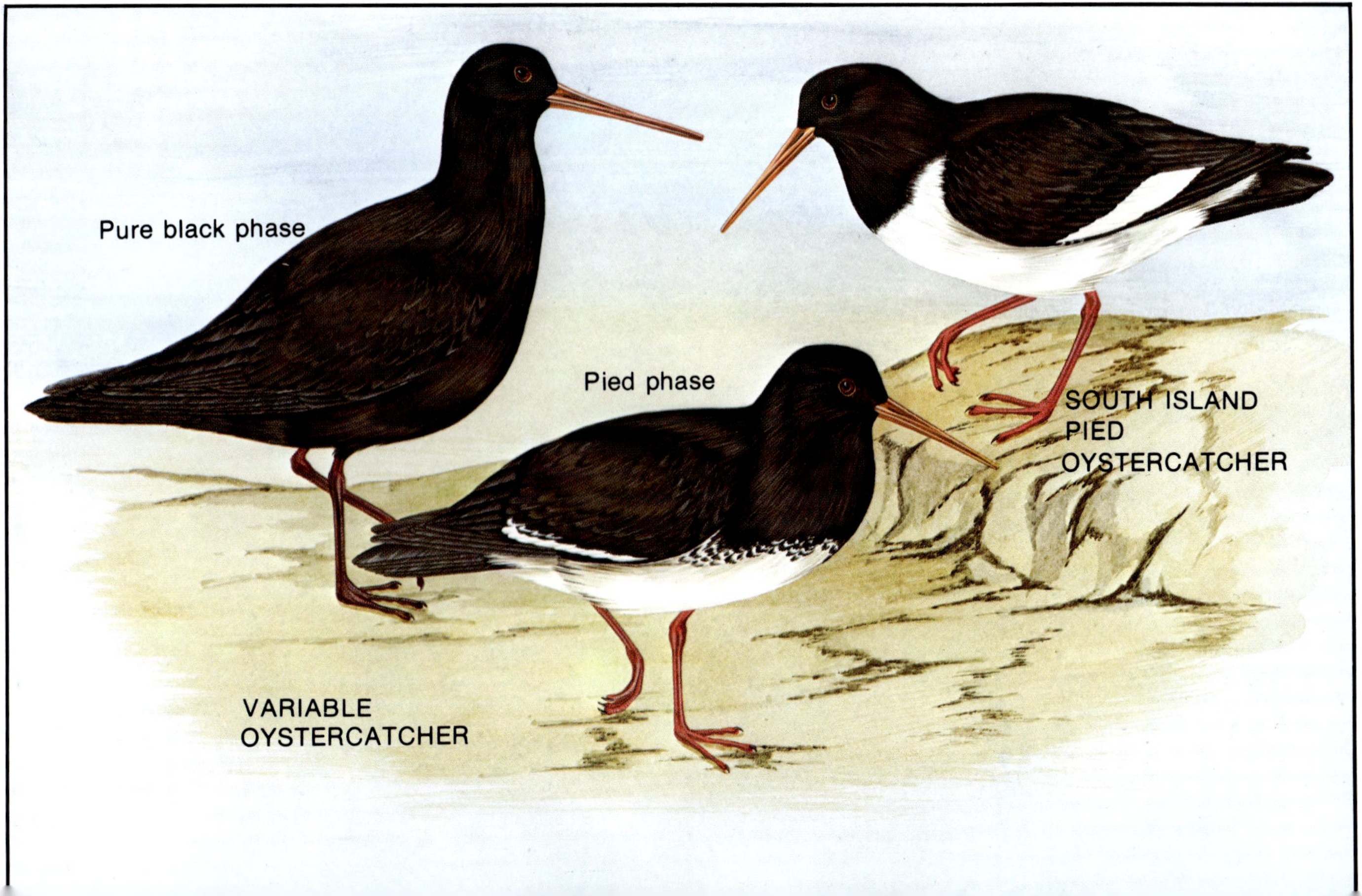
Pure black phase
Pied phase
SOUTH ISLAND PIED OYSTERCATCHER
VARIABLE OYSTERCATCHER

South Island Pied Oystercatcher (Torea)

Haematopus ostralegus
Family: HAEMATOPODIDAE

Plate 30

Native: Similar sub-species also in Australia, South America and Northern Hemisphere. (Fully protected.)

Field Characters:
— conspicuous, black upper parts sharply separated from white below.
— white of breast extending above and in front of closed wing.
— in flight, prominent broad white wing stripe and white back from rump to shoulders.

Distribution and Habitat:
— breeds inland on South Island riverbeds and surrounding farmlands, east of main divide.
— from January to August found on coast throughout New Zealand in large flocks mainly on estuaries, mudflats and wet paddocks.
— feeds on crustacea, shellfish, worms and larvae.

Breeding:
September to November.
— Nest: scrape mainly in river sand or shingle.
— Eggs: 2-3, variable from pale brown to cream with dark brown and black spots and blotches all over.

Variable Oystercatcher (Torea-pango)

Haematopus unicolour
Family: HAEMATOPODIDAE

Plate 30

Endemic: (Fully protected.)

Field Characters:
— larger than South Island Pied Oystercatcher.
— 2 basic colour phases: *"Pure Black"*, and *"Pied"*. The latter differs from South Island Pied by smudgy separation between black and white on underside and *no white on shoulder in front of wing.*
— narrow white wing stripe, and white only on *lower* back.
— many birds show intermediate plumages between both above phases and pairs may consist of both phases.

Distribution and Habitat:
— Only on beaches and coast throughout New Zealand and many offshore islands.
— feeds on shellfish, crustacea and worms.

(Continued on page 65)

SPUR-WINGED PLOVER

Spur-winged Plover

Vanellus miles
Family: CHARADRIIDAE

Plate 31

Native: Straggling from Australia since 1886 and breeding since 1940s. (Fully protected.)

Field Characters:
— pigeon size.
— sexes the same.
— slow flapping wing beat.
— crown and shoulders black, back brown, white below.
— distinctive yellow facial wattles.
— loud "rattling" call.

Distribution and Habitat:
— have expanded range throughout New Zealand, but most common in south.
— pasture and low crops, often near swamps, water courses and on seashore.
— flocks in autumn.
— feeds on worms and insects.

Breeding:
— July to December.
— Nest: a scrape or hollow in ground with virtually no nest material.
— Eggs: 3-4, muddy-green with variable blotching of purplish-brown all over.

(Continued from page 63)
Breeding:
— October to January.
— Nest: scrape in beach sand or shingle.
— Eggs: 2-3, stone-buff spotted and blotched with dark brown.

BANDED DOTTEREL

♂

♀

Immature

Plate 32

Banded Dotterel
(Tuturiwhatu)

Charadrius bicinctus
Family: CHARADRIIDAE

Endemic: A related sub-species in Auckland Islands south of New Zealand. (Fully protected.)

Field Characters:
— size similar to Song Thrush.
— dumpy bird with very short tail.
— Female: colours of bands less intense and *no* black forehead above white stripe.
— Immature and Winter Adult: bands on breast and black stripe on face *absent.*
— short rushing runs, bobbing movements when stopped.
— high pitched staccato "pit pit" call.

Distribution and Habitat:
— throughout New Zealand on coasts, riverbeds and lake shores.
— following breeding, inland birds move to coast, while there is a general northwind movement and concentration in northern New Zealand in winter.
— some, probably immature birds, move across Tasman to winter in Australia.

Breeding:
— August to December.
— Nest: scrape in sand or shingle rarely with nesting material.
— Eggs: normally 3, greyish or greenish closely marked with dark brown or black spots and blotches all over.

BLACK-FRONTED DOTTEREL

Black-fronted Dotterel

Charadrius melanops
Family: CHARADRIIDAE

Plate 33

Native: Australia, self-introduced 1950s. (Fully protected.)

Field Characters:
— smaller than Banded Dotterel.
— striking black and white design on head.
— broad black Y-shaped band on breast, not present in Immature.
— chestnut-brown patch on shoulder.
— voice is high-pitched whistle or soft "Tink Tink".

Distribution and Habitat:
— first seen Hawke's Bay and now common in Central Hawke's Bay, shingle riverbeds, spreading to Wairarapa, Manawatu and east coast of South Island.
— in New Zealand breeding on riverbeds generally not far inland, but in Australia is mainly inland on edges of stagnant water.
— feeds on aquatic insects and invertebrates.

Breeding:
— September to January.
— Nest: generally a scrape among grass and shingle sometimes in open.
— Eggs: normally 3, yellowish-stone heavily spotted and marked all over with dark brown.

WRYBILL

Breeding

Non-breeding

Wrybill
(Ngutu parore)

Anarhynchus frontalis
Family: CHARADRIIDAE

Plate 34

Endemic: (Fully protected.)

Field Characters:
— somewhat smaller than Banded Dotterel.
— uniform light grey above.
— pure white below with black "collar" in breeding plumage only.
— bill black, long, pointed, and tip bent to right side.

Distribution and Habitat:
— breeds on South Island broad shingle riverbeds east of main divide in Canterbury and North Otago.
— from December to July on mudflats and estuaries, the majority migrating to the Auckland area but smaller numbers may be found elsewhere.
— feeds on insects and small invertebrates.

Breeding:
— September to November.
— Nest: small scrape in river sand or shingle.
— Eggs: normally 2, light grey evenly covered with minute dark spots.

Breeding

Non-breeding

EASTERN BAR-TAILED GODWIT

Eastern Bar-tailed Godwit
(Kuaka)

Limosa lapponica
Family: SCOLOPACIDAE

Plate 35

Migrant: From North-east Siberia and Alaska. Closely related subspecies in North Europe. (Fully protected.)

Field Characters:
— body smaller than Oystercatcher.
— long black slender legs.
— long slightly upturned bill.
— "Non-Breeding" plumage generally mottled greyish-buff from September to February.
— "Breeding" plumage starting to appear in February except for Immature which retain non-breeding plumage throughout first year.

Distribution and Habitat:
— arrive in New Zealand in September and majority depart in late March. Some non-breeding birds remain here during our winter.
— found mainly in flocks on coastal marshes and mudflats throughout New Zealand with concentrations in Auckland, Farewell Spit, Christchurch and Invercargill.
— feeds on small marine invertebrates, crustacea and molluscs.

Breeding:
— May to June.
— nesting in North-east Siberia and Alaska.
— Eggs: normally 4, large greenish-brown with dark brown blotches.

PIED STILT

Pied Stilt
(Poaka)

Himantopus himantopus
Family: RECURVIROSTRIDAE

Plate 36

Native: Throughout world in temperate and tropical regions. (Fully protected.)

Field Characters:
— striking black and white plumage.
— long spindly pink legs, trailing far beyond tail in flight.
— long straight awl-like bill.
— monotonous yapping call.
— Immature: back of neck *grey* and often with dark smudges round eye.

Distribution and Habitat:
— common throughout New Zealand anywhere there is water up to 1,000 m.
— on lake edges, marshes, wet paddocks and riverbeds, moving from inland areas to coast in autumn.
— feeds on aquatic insects, worms, snails and shellfish.

Breeding:
— September to January.
— Nest: from scrapes in shingle, lined with a little grass to substantial nests with variable amounts of grass and weeds, on ground close to or surrounded by shallow water.
— mostly in open but sometimes in clumps of grass.
— Eggs: normally 4, from buff to olive-brown heavily marked all over with black and brown spots and blotches.

Note: The Black Stilt *(Himantopus novaezealandiae)* is very rare, breeding only within the Waitaki Basin system in South Canterbury and Otago. Mixed pairs of Black and Pied Stilts can occur.

SOUTHERN BLACK-BACKED GULL

Adult

Second year

First year

Southern Black-backed Gull
(Karoro)

Larus dominicanus
Family: LARIDAE

Plate 37

Native: Circumpolar in southern temperate to sub-antarctic regions. (Not protected.)

Field Characters:
— largest of 3 New Zealand gulls.
— Adult: black and white, with white tips to flight feathers and *pure white tail.*
— First Year: mottled greyish-brown with *dark* bill.
— Second Year: very variable, ranging from close to first year to adult with no white tips to flight feathers and some *black* in tail.

Distribution and Habitat:
— throughout New Zealand on or near coast far inland to farmland and even alpine regions.
— feeds on any accessible animal food, often entirely by scavenging.
— commonly seen in large flocks frequenting rubbish dumps, riverbeds and fields.

Breeding:
— October to December.
— Nest: fairly bulky collection of grasses and other plants often pulled up by roots.
— may be singly or in large colonies.
— Eggs: normally 3, variable from light blue to dark olive-brown with brown and black spots and blotches.

RED-BILLED GULL

Adult

Immature

Red-billed Gull
(Tarapunga)

Larus novaehollandiae
Family: LARIDAE

Plate 38

Native: Also related sub-species in Australia and South Africa. (Fully protected.)

Field Characters:
— half-size of Black-backed Gull.
— white body, pearly grey back, black wing feathers tipped with white.
— Adult: short red bill, bright red legs, feet and eye ring.
— Immature: dark brown to brownish-red bill, purplish brown legs and feet, brown spots on back and wing coverts (these spots not generally present after July of first winter).

Distribution and Habitat:
— throughout New Zealand especially on coasts and offshore islands, occasionally inland.
— often in large flocks.
— feeds on small fish, crustacea, worms, sometimes berries, and also scavenging on dead animal matter.

Breeding:
— October to December.
— Nest: of seaweed, grasses and ice plant, in tight colonies from a few to thousands of birds, on islands, rocky headlands, cliffs and beaches.
— Eggs: 2-3, colour variable grey to brown with light and dark brown blotches all over.

BLACK-BILLED GULL

Immature

Black-billed Gull
(Tarapunga)

Larus bulleri
Family: LARIDAE

Plate 39

Endemic: (Fully protected.)

Field Characters:
— similar in size to Red-billed Gull.
— in flight the mainly white outer flight feathers distinguish it from the Red-billed Gull who has mainly black feathers.
— Adult: bill, *black,* more slender and longer than Red-billed Gull, legs and feet reddish-black.
— Immature: similar to immature Red-billed Gull but having longer bill which is pinkish or orange with black tip.

Distribution and Habitat:
— breeding mainly in South Island on larger shingle riverbeds.
— Uncommon in North Island, but regular colonies at Rotorua, Hawke's Bay, and Poverty Bay.
— following breeding season inland birds move to coast and there is also a northward movement across Cook Strait.
— feeds on aquatic and land insects, often seen in freshly ploughed fields, also scavenging in towns during winter.

Breeding:
— October to December.
— Nest: of grasses and other plant matter in tight colonies.
— Eggs: 2-3, similar to Red-billed Gull, but generally lighter in colour.

BLACK-FRONTED TERN

Black-fronted Tern
(Tara)

Sterna albostriata
Family: STERNIDAE

Plate 40

Endemic: (Fully protected.)

Field Characters:
— small grey tern, with black cap and white stripe under eye.
— bill and feet bright orange.
— white rump noticeable in flight.
— Immature: head speckled brown, darkest on nape, bill dark brown.
— call a high-pitched staccato whistling at intervals, with harsh "yark" near breeding colony.

Distribution and Habitat:
— only breeding South Island, inland on shingle riverbeds east of main ranges.
— during the winter move to coast, also to North Island in small numbers.
— feeds on small fish, water insects and larvae, may "hawk" for caterpillars, flying insects and moths. Commonly seen following plough or harrows during cultivation of fields.

Breeding:
— October to January.
— Nest: scrape in sand or shingle in loose colonies sometimes associated with Black-billed Gulls.
— Eggs: 1-3, variable from dark stone to light-brown with large light or dark brown blotches all over.

CASPIAN TERN

Caspian Tern
(Taranui)

Hydroprogne caspia
Family: STERNIDAE

Plate 41

Native: Throughout world in tropical and temperate zone. (Fully protected.)

Field Characters:
— very large tern, bigger than Red-billed Gull.
— light grey above, white below.
— black cap and feet, large red bill.
— Immature: with mottled cap similar to adult outside breeding season.
— over water, downward pointing head in flight.
— voice is a raucous drawn-out "kaah".

Distribution and Habitat:
— North and South Island, more plentiful in north.
— generally singly or in pairs frequenting coastal estuaries and penetrating inland along rivers to major lakes.
— feeds on small fish by plunge diving.

Breeding:
— September to January.
— Nest: scrape in sand or shingle mainly in colonies on shingle banks, sandy beaches and dunes.
— isolated nests on rocky promontories.
— occasionally inland near fresh-water lakes.
— Eggs: 1-3, light stone with dark brown spots and blotches.

WHITE-FRONTED TERN

White-fronted Tern
(Tara)

Sterna striata
Family: STERNIDAE

Plate 42

Endemic: (Fully protected.)

Field Characters:
— size between Caspian and Black-fronted Tern.
— silver-grey above, white below, bill and feet black.
— large black cap and white stripe (much extended in winter) on forehead.
— deeply forked light grey tail.
— Juvenile: cap lightly mottled with brown or buff, back and wings barred with black stripes.

Distribution and Habitat:
— throughout New Zealand mainly on coast.
— many juveniles cross Tasman and spend at least their first winter on the east Australian coast. Breeding recorded in Bass Strait.
— feeds mainly on shoaling small fish by plunge diving from the air.

Breeding:
— October to January.
— Nest: on bare rock or scrape in sand or shingle, but sometimes of variable amounts of grasses, twigs and iceplant.
— in colonies of a few to several hundred often associated with Red-billed Gulls.
— Eggs: 1-2, variable light stone, green or brown with small scattered light and dark brown blotches.

NEW ZEALAND PIGEON

New Zealand Pigeon
(Kereru)

Hemiphaga novaeseelandiae
Family: COLUMBIDAE

Plate 43

Endemic: One closely related sub-species in the Chatham Islands. (Fully protected.)

Field Characters:
— large, distinctively coloured irridescent green with coppery reflections, white underparts.
— heavy flight with loud swishing of wings.
— spectacular rising and falling nuptial flights in spring.

Distribution and Habitat:
— throughout New Zealand, can occur in towns, though now mainly restricted to native bush. Unfortunately in some districts poaching still occurs.
— feeds on young leaves, the flowers and fruits of native trees.
— has adapted to introduced plants and feeds on tree lucerne, clover, willows and plums etc.

Breeding:
— mainly November to January.
— Nest: flimsy structure of twigs in trees and shrubs.
— Eggs: 1, pure white.

ROCK PIGEON

Rock Pigeon

Columba livia
Family: COLUMBIDAE

Plate 44

Introduced: As domesticated races and now wild. (Not protected.)

Field Characters:
— because of the number of original breeds, a widely variable range of plumages from white to black is seen.
— in wild flocks many now reverting to original plumage characters shown in the plate.

Distribution and Habitat:
— throughout New Zealand especially along east coast and in major towns and cities.
— also cliffs, clay banks, seashore and riverbeds.
— feeds mainly on seeds.

Breeding:
— throughout the year.
— Nest: flimsy, of light sticks, on buildings and ledges, and in cliff crannies.
— Eggs: generally 2, pure white.

KEA

SOUTH ISLAND KAKA

Kaka

Nestor meridionalis
Family: NESTORIDAE

Plate 45

Endemic: Two closely related sub-species, one in North Island and one in Southern Islands. (Fully protected.)

Field Characters:
— somewhat smaller than New Zealand Piegon.
— large hooked bill.
— light crown and nape, bright scarlet underwing.
— North Island sub-species, greyer on crown, less red on belly, more chocolate-brown than green in general colour.
— voice a raucous "ka-aa" and melodious whistle.

Distribution and Habitat:
— mainly confined to larger areas of native bush and some offshore island sanctuaries, e.g. Kapiti and Little Barrier Island.
— rarely into exotic plantations and gardens.
— feeds on nectar, berries, grubs and seeds.

Breeding:
— November to January.
— Nest: in hollow trees without nest material.
— Eggs: 4–5, white.

Kea

Nestor notabilis
Family: NESTORIDAE

Plate 45

Endemic: (Fully protected.)

Field Characters:
— size similar to Kaka.
— mainly olive-green with orange-red on rump and under wing.
— harsh "kee-a" call mainly in flight.

Distribution and Habitat:
— generally only in South Island high country from Marlborough-Nelson to Fiordland, but reaching coast during winter in Nelson and Westland.
— most commonly seen above bushline, but also present in native bush.
— feeds on roots, leaves, buds, fruits, insects and nectar.

(Continued on page 95)

EASTERN ROSELLA

Eastern Rosella

Platycercus eximius
Family: **PLATYCERCIDAE**

Introduced: From cage-escaped birds. Also found in Eastern Australia. (Not protected.)

Field Characters:
— twice size of Parakeet.
— strikingly and brilliantly coloured.
— very rapid wing beat in flight.
— prominent long tail.

Distribution and Habitat:
— common in native bush north of the the Waikato, also western Wairarapa, Upper Hutt Valley and Dunedin.
— feeds on berries, seeds, flowers, and occasionally fruit.

Breeding:
— nests in holes in hollow branches or trees. Further details unknown in New Zealand.
— In Australia breeds from August to January.
— Eggs: 4–7, white.
— female only incubates.

(Continued from page 93)
Breeding:
— August to December.
— Nest: on ground in crevices or holes in logs, occasionally with twigs and leaves for nesting material.
— Eggs: 2–4, white.

RED-CROWNED PARAKEET

YELLOW-CROWNED PARAKEET

Red-crowned Parakeet (Kakariki)

Cyanoramphus novaezelandiae
Family: PLATYCERCIDAE

Plate 47

Native: Also New Caledonia. Several closely related sub-species in New Zealand region. (Fully protected.)

Field Characters:
— small parrot, size of Blackbird.
— red forehead and crown.
— red patch *behind* eye.
— rapid wing beat, swift straight flight.
— chattering call mainly when in flight.

Distribution and Habitat:
— some large areas of native bush on mainland, but more plentiful on outlying islands.
— feeds on wide variety of vegetable matter from fruits and seeds to leaves and buds.
— commonly held in aviaries under permit.

Breeding:
— October to March.
— Nest: deposits eggs in hollow trees and rock crevices.
— Eggs: 4–9, white.
— female only incubates.

Yellow-crowned Parakeet (Kakariki)

Cyanoramphus auriceps
Family: PLATYCERCIDAE

Plate 47

Endemic: Two closely related sub-species. (Fully protected.)

Field Characters:
— smaller than Red-crowned Parakeet.
— red forehead, *yellow* crown.
— no red behind eye.
— flight and call similar to Red-crowned Parakeet.

Distribution and Habitat:
— similar to Red-crowned Parakeet, but more plentiful and widespread on the mainland.
— food similar to Red-crowned Parakeet.
— commonly held in aviaries under permit.

Breeding:
— August to April.
— Nest and Eggs: as for Red-crowned Parakeet.
— female only incubates.

LONG-TAILED CUCKOO

SHINING CUCKOO

Shining Cuckoo
(Pipiwharauroa)

Chrysococcyx lucidus
Family: CUCULIDAE

Native (Migratory): Only breeding in New Zealand. (Fully protected.)

Field Characters:
— size of House Sparrow.
— more often heard than seen.
— Female and Immature: duller and with less distinct bars on cheeks.
— voice, a musical series of double notes with downward slur at end of call.

Distribution and Habitat:
— throughout New Zealand up to 1,200 m.
— arriving in August, migrating north in February to Solomon Islands and Bismark Archipelago.
— feeds on insects and caterpillars.

Breeding:
— October to January.
— lays eggs in nest of mainly Grey Warbler, but also Fantail, Tit, and Silvereye.
— Eggs: 1 per nest of host, total number per season unknown, greenish or bluish-white to olive-brown.
— when chick hatches, eggs or chicks of host are ejected by foster chick.

Long-tailed Cuckoo
(Koekoea)

Eudynamys taitensis
Family: CUCULIDAE

Native (Migratory): Only breeding in New Zealand. (Fully protected.)

Field Characters:
— bigger than Blackbird, tail longer than body.
— Immature: differ by being greyish-brown speckled all over above with pale spots, undersides reddish-buff with fine dark streaks.
— voice, long harsh piercing screech.

Distribution and Habitat:
— throughout New Zealand arriving in September to October, migrating north in February to South-west Pacific Islands.
— feeds on insects, lizards, young birds and eggs.

(Continued on page 101)

MOREPORK

Morepork
(Ruru)

Ninox novaeseelandiae
Family: STRIGIDAE

Native: Also Australia and New Guinea. (Fully protected.)

Field Characters:
— generally nocturnal and usually heard rather than seen.
— voice, clear almost "quor-coo" with falling second syllable. Also harsh and vibrating screech.

Distribution and Habitat:
— throughout New Zealand in native and introduced forest, also close to settlement in parks and gardens.
— often seen at late dusk on prominent perch or hawking for food.
— feeds mainly on moths and insects including wetas, also lizards, mice, rats, and small birds.

Breeding:
— October to November.
— Nest: generally in hollow trees, but also in dense clumps of vegetation, rarely in open.
— Eggs: 2–3, white.
— female only incubates and broods chicks.

(Continued from page 99)

Breeding:
— November to December.
— lays eggs in nest of mainly Whitehead and Brown Creeper, but also Yellowhead, Tit, Robin, Silvereye.
— Eggs: 1 per nest of host, total number per season unknown, creamy-white spotted and blotched all over with purplish-brown and grey.
— eggs and chicks of host ejected as with Shining Cuckoo.

LITTLE OWL

Little Owl

Athene noctua
Family: STRIGIDAE

Plate 50

Introduced: Originally from Germany to Otago, 1906. (Partially protected.)

Field Characters:
— smaller and lighter in colour than Morepork.,
— only owl seen flying and hunting in daylight.
— dipping flight.
— rounded head and wings.

Distribution and Habitat:
— South Island except for mountain ranges, sightings in North Island not confirmed.
— open country and forest edges.
— often seen sitting on fence posts.
— feeds mainly on mice, insects and earthworms, occasionally small birds and lizards.

Breeding:
— September to December.
— Nest: in hollow trees, holes in banks or buildings and occasionally in deserted rabbit burrows. No nest material.
— Eggs: 2–5, round and pure white.

KINGFISHER

Kingfisher
(Kotare)

Halcyon sancta
Family: ALCEDINIDAE

Plate 51

Native: Also Australia. (Fully protected.)

Field Characters:
— bright greenish-blue above and off-white to buff below.
— large black pointed bill.
— very short legs.
— direct flight.
— Immature birds: duller in colour with darker mottled breast.

Distribution and Habitat:
— common throughout New Zealand especially in the north.
— wide range of habitat including seashore, open country, bush edges, entering bush along water courses.
— can often be seen perching on power and telephone lines as vantage point.
— feeds by swooping on prey from high perch, mainly mice, lizards, insects, crabs, worms and occasionally dives for small fish.

Breeding:
— October to January.
— Nest: in holes in trees and clay banks dug by the birds. No nest material.
— Eggs: 4–5, shining pure white.

RIFLEMAN

♂

♀

Rifleman
(Titipounamu)

Acanthisitta chloris
Family: XENICIDAE

Plate 52

Endemic: Two closely related sub-species one in North Island and one in Southern Islands. (Fully protected).

Field Characters:
— smallest of New Zealand birds.
— Male: mainly green above.
— Female: streaked buff and dark brown above.
— tail black, tipped with buff and very short.
— continuously on move with vigorous wing flicking when on branches and tree trunks.
— voice, irregular very high pitched "zipt-zipt-zipt".

Distribution and Habitat:
— throughout New Zealand except north of Te Aroha, but also Great and Little Barrier Islands.
— in native and exotic forest up to bushline.
— feeds mainly on insects, small larvae and moths high in trees by searching among bark and foliage.

Breeding:
— August to January, generally 2 broods.
— Nest: closely woven of fine roots and leaves lined with feathers in hollow limbs, bark crevices and clay banks.
— Eggs: 2–4, white.

ROCK WREN

Rock Wren

Xenicus gilviventris
Family: XENICIDAE

Plate 53

Endemic: (Fully protected.)

Field Characters:
— between Silvereye and House Sparrow in size.
— very short tail, disproportionately large feet.
— rarely flies more than a few yards.
— frequent vigorous bobbing of body.
— often heard underfoot in rock piles.

Distribution and Habitat:
— only in South Island from Nelson to Fiordland.
— alpine and sub-alpine generally above scrubline, on or in rock falls and crevices.
— feeds actively on and under ground mainly on insects and spiders.

Breeding:
— September to November.
— Nest: in rock crevices or holes between rocks, a bulky igloo-shaped structure woven from snow tussock and may be generously lined with feathers.
— Eggs: 2–5, white.

SKYLARK

NEW ZEALAND PIPIT

Skylark

Alauda arvensis
Family: ALAUDIDAE

Introduced: From Europe, 1864 onwards. (Not protected.)

Field Characters:
— marked crest often raised when startled.
— can be confused with New Zealand Pipit, but has long trilling song mainly while flying.
— rapid wing beats while ascending in a spiral to considerable heights and then slowly descending.
— noticeably longer and straighter hind claw than Pipit.

Distribution and Habitat:
— plentiful throughout New Zealand.
— all types of open country up to high altitude but not alpine.
— feeds mainly on seeds and insects.

Breeding:
— October to January, more than one brood.
— Nest: in ground hollows, a neat grass lined cup well concealed in taller grasses and rushes.
— Eggs: 3–7, yellowish-cream thickly blotched all over with brown and grey, often forming circle at larger end.

New Zealand Pipit
(Pihoihoi)

Anthus novaeseelandiae
Family: MOTACILLIDAE

Native: Very similar species throughout world. (Fully protected.)

Field Characters:
— similar to Skylark, without crest and greyer in colour, pale eye stripe more prominent, often flicks tail.
— a 'pi-pit' call commonly from low perch.

Distribution and Habitat:
— throughout New Zealand in open or scrub country up to alpine. Often at roadside and on beaches.
— feeds mainly on insects, worms, rarely seeds.

Breeding:
— August to March, more than one brood.
— Nest: on ground, substantial deep cup lined with dry grass, well concealed under vegetation.
— Eggs: 3–4, cream, heavy blotches of brown and grey often concealing cream.

WELCOME SWALLOW

Welcome Swallow

Hirundo tahitica
Family: HIRUNDINIDAE

Plate 55

Native: S.W. Pacific and Australia, self-introduced, rare straggler prior to 1950s, still spreading. (Fully protected.)

Field Characters:
— smaller than House Sparrow.
— glossy bluish-black with chestnut face and throat.
— strongly forked tail.
— swift erratic flight.

Distribution and Habitat:
— throughout both islands, more plentiful in North.
— open country close to water, breeding commonly under bridges.
— often seen perching on wires and bare branches.
— gathers in flocks near water in autumn and winter.
— feeds on small flying insects, often above open water.

Breeding:
— September to February, more than one brood.
— Nest: composed of mud pellets reinforced with grass, a shallow cup lined with feathers, attached to a rough vertical surface.
— Eggs: 3–5, white, freckled with chestnut spots.

HEDGE SPARROW

Hedge Sparrow

Prunella modularis
Family: PRUNELLIDAE

Plate 56

Introduced: Originally 1868 from Europe. (Not protected.)

Field Characters:
— inconspicuous and seemingly solitary.
— similar in size to House Sparrow, but slimmer.
— blue-grey on breast, streaked brown on back, sexes similar.
— moves in short hops with body inclined forward, and flicking movements of wings and raised tail.
— never high above ground except male on song perch.
— short straight flight.

Distribution and Habitat:
— common throughout New Zealand.
— mainly gardens, hedges, scrubland, forest edges and clearings.
— feeds on insects and small seeds.

Breeding:
— August to January, more than one brood.
— Nest: very close to ground in thick cover, neatly lined with mosses, fine grass, hair, occasionally wool.
— Eggs: 3–5, pure intensive turquoise-blue.

FERNBIRD

Plate 57

Fernbird
(Matata)

Bowdleria punctata
Family: MUSCICAPIDAE

Endemic: Five sub-species, one extinct. (Fully protected.)

Field Characters:
— very inconspicuous, mostly in pairs.
— reluctant and poor flier.
— flies with markedly drooping tail.
— untidy tail.
— distinctive sharp metallic call "plik-plik" made by pairs calling to each other.

Distribution and Habitat:
— throughout New Zealand, but becoming localised through loss of habitat.
— swamps, wetlands, bracken and scrublands, not alpine.
— feeds on insects.

Breeding:
— September to February.
— Nest: neatly woven of rushes and grasses, a deep cup lined with feathers, well concealed a few inches from ground or above stagnant water.
— Eggs: 2–3, pinkish-white, with brown dots all over and concentrated near larger end.

BROWN CREEPER

Brown Creeper
(Pipipi)

Finschia novaeseelandiae
Family: MUSCICAPIDAE

Endemic: (Fully protected.)

Field Characters:
— smaller than House Sparrow.
— generally brown above and light buff below.
— feeds in noisy flocks.

Distribution and Habitat:
— only South Island, Stewart Island and their offlying islands.
— mostly in native bush, but also in exotic plantations and scrub.
— not in open country.
— up to but not including sub-alpine.
— feeds on insects, moths and grubs.

Breeding:
— November to January.
— Nest: neat cup woven of grass fibres and moss, lined with feathers, well hidden in tops of shrubs.
— Eggs: 3–4, white, heavily blotched with brown and purplish-brown more dense at large end.
— female only incubates.
— often a host to Long-tailed Cuckoo.

WHITEHEAD

Plate 59

Whitehead
(Popokatea)

Mohoua albicilla
Family: MUSCICAPIDAE

Endemic: (Fully protected.)

Field Characters:
— size similar to Silvereye.
— dull brown above, head and underparts white slightly tinged with brown, female duller on head.
— except for breeding season is seen in noisy flocks.
— voice, hard single "zit".

Distribution and Habitat:
— only North Island and associated large offshore islands.
— locally plentiful from Te Aroha, Pirongia and East Cape southwards.
— in native bush and major exotic forests.
— feeds on insects in forest canopy, tree trunks and logs, also seeds and small soft fruits.

Breeding:
— October to February.
— Nest: bulky, cup-shaped nest of twigs, rootlets, grass and bark bound with spiders' web, lined with bark in canopy of shrubs or low trees.
— Eggs: 2–4, translucent white, variably spotted with brown or reddish-brown.
— often host to Long-tailed Cuckoo.

YELLOWHEAD

♂

♀

Yellowhead
(Mohoua)

Mohoua ochrocephala
Family: MUSCICAPIDAE

Plate 60

Endemic: (Fully protected.)

Field Characters:
— size of House Sparrow.
— olive-green above with canary yellow head and chest.
— Female and Immature: have less yellow on nape.
— except for breeding season seen in flocks or family groups.
— voice, a musical canary-like call and a high pitched buzzing.

Distribution and Habitat:
— locally common in South Island beech forest.
— frequents dense native forest canopy and does not move into scrub areas like Brown Creeper.
— feeds on insects in foliage and in debris collected in tree forks and bark, occasionally on ground.

Breeding:
— November to December.
— Nest: cup-shaped of moss, rootlets and spiders' web lined with fine grass in natural holes in dead trees.
— Eggs: 3–4, pinkish-white, evenly blotched with reddish-brown.
— female only incubates.
— sometimes host to Long-tailed Cuckoo.

GREY WARBLER

Grey Warbler
(Riroriro)

Gerygone igata
Family: MUSCICAPIDAE

Plate 61

Endemic: Related species in the Chatham Islands. (Fully protected.)

Field Characters:
— smaller than Silvereye.
— conspicuous white tip to tail in flight.
— more commonly heard than seen.
— song, a penetrating high melodious rising and falling trill.
— very active, always on move from perch to perch, often hovers near outside foliage when in search of food.

Distribution and Habitat:
— common throughout New Zealand.
— absent from open country and alpine areas.
— feeds mainly on spiders, insects and their larvae.

Breeding:
— August to December, usually two clutches.
— Nest: hanging pear-shaped structure with side entrance; constructed of grasses, moss, and spiders' web, well lined with feathers.
— Eggs: 3–5, pinkish-white, dotted all over with brown.
— female only incubates.

Note: Favourite host of Shining Cuckoo, who lays its egg with second clutch and leaves the warbler to incubate the egg and rear the chick.

Plate 61

FANTAIL "North Island"

"Black" phase

Fantail
(Piwakawaka)

Rhipidura fuliginosa
Family: MUSCICAPIDAE

Native: Also Australia and the Pacific, with three closely related sub-species in New Zealand. (Fully protected.)

Field Characters:
— smaller than House Sparrow.
— chubby body, long tail often fanned.
— erratic butterfly-like flight.
— two colour phases, the "black" phase rare in North Island.
— white ear patch in "black" phase not always present.

Distribution and Habitat:
— throughout New Zealand.
— common in any habitat with trees and shrubs.
— often in small flocks or family groups.
— feeds on insects, especially by "hawking".

Breeding:
— August to January, more than one brood.
— Nest: small firm cup of fibres, moss, bark and hair, coated with spiders' web, with neat fine fibre lining. Often has loose material hanging from base forming a "beard".
— 2–6 m from ground, usually on a slender branch of horizontal fork, often above water.
— Eggs: 3–4, white with grey and brown spots more dense at larger end.

TIT

Yellow-breasted ♂

♀

Pied ♂

Tit
(Miro miro, Ngiru ngiru)

Petroica macrocephala
Family: MUSCICAPIDAE

Plate 63

Endemic: Five closely related sub-species with Pied and Yellow-breasted Tit illustrated in plate. (Fully protected.)

Field Characters:
— size between House Sparrow and Silvereye.
— Female: as shown, for both sub-species, but may have slightly yellower undersides in Yellow-breasted Tit.
— Male *Pied:* black and white.
— Male *Yellow-breasted:* yellow undersides varying from pale yellow to orange-yellow with bright orange stripe at chest margin of black and yellow.
— both sexes have prominent white patch on wing, especially seen when in flight.
— song is a cheerful often repeated trill.

Distribution and Habitat:
— throughout New Zealand, with Pied in North Island, Yellow-breasted in South Island.
— in native and exotic forest.
— feeds on grubs and insects often caught in flight.

Breeding:
— September to February, 2 broods.
— Nest: of moss, bark and cobwebs lined with feathers, located in hollow in tree trunk, rock crevice or sometimes in branch fork up to 10 m.
— Eggs: 3–4, cream, light yellowish and purplish-brown spots densest at larger end.
— female only incubates.

ROBIN   North Island

♂

South Island

♂

♀

Robin
(Toutouwai)

Petroica australis
Family: MUSCICAPIDAE

Plate 64

Endemic: Three closely related sub-species with North and South Island forms illustrated. (Fully protected.)

Field Characters:
— smaller than Starling, bigger than House Sparrow.
— Male: *sooty-black*, with white streaks on head and throat, white belly and undertail.
— Female: slightly browner above with light cream belly and undertail.
— *South Island:*
— Male: *dusky-black.* lower breast, belly and undertail cream-buff.
— Female: slightly browner above.
— strikingly long legs.
— very tame and inquisitive.

Distribution and Habitat:
— now irregularly throughout New Zealand, but localised, in some areas.
— in both native and exotic forest.
— feeds on insects and small worms in lower levels of forest and on ground.

Breeding:
— August to February.
— Nest: rather bulky, of moss, bark and roots bound with spiders' web lined with tree fern scales and soft grasses.
— in tree hollows, rock crevices and tree forks relatively lower than Tit.
— Eggs: 2–4, cream, with purplish-brown spots denser at larger end.
— female only incubates.

SONG THRUSH

Song Thrush

Turdus philomelos
Family: MUSCICAPIDAE

Introduced: From Europe 1860s. (Not protected.)

Field Characters:
— sexes similar.
— uniform olive-brown above, undersides light buff with bold dark brown spots on breast and flank.
— belly white.
— loud and rapid alarm call "tchik-tchik".

Distribution and Habitat:
— fairly common throughout New Zealand.
— not inside heavy bush, or alpine.
— feeds mostly on ground on snails, worms, insects, also berries and small fruit.

Breeding:
— June to January, more than one clutch.
— Nest: generally low and often conspicuous, big nest of twigs, roots, grasses and mud, the deep cup smoothly lined with wood pulp (mixture of rotten wood and saliva).
— Eggs: 3–5, clear blue with scattered black spots chiefly at larger end.

BLACKBIRD ♂

♀

Blackbird

Turdus merula
Family: MUSCICAPIDAE

Plate 66

Introduced: From Europe 1860s. (Not protected.)

Field Characters:
— Male: glossy black with bright yellow bill.
— Female: uniform dark brown above, lighter below with inconspicuous streaks on throat, lightly spotted breast, grey chin, bill generally brown.
— Immature: dark brown with buff streaking on back and rusty brown undersides with dark streaks and speckles.
— partial or total albinos occur.
— voice mellower than song thrush and alarm call a persistant "tchink tchink".

Distribution and Habitat:
— very common throughout New Zealand.
— all habitats except alpine.
— feeds mainly on ground on worms and often fruit.

Breeding:
— July to January, more than one clutch.
— Nest: often conspicuous on trees, shrubs, hedges, and frequently on or in buildings; big and often untidy of grasses, roots and fibres bound with mud. Deep cup lined with grass and rootlets.
— Eggs: 2–4, dull turquoise, thickly freckled with red-brown.

SILVEREYE

Plate 67

Silvereye
(Tauhou)

Zosterops lateralis
Family: ZOSTEROPIDAE

Native: Also S.E. Australia, self-introduced mid-1800s. (Partially protected.)

Field Characters:
— smaller than House Sparrow.
— distinctive white eye ring.
— bright yellowish-green above with grey saddle, light grey breast and rusty flanks.
— most obvious in winter when moving in flocks.

Distribution and Habitat:
— throughout New Zealand.
— all areas with tree cover including subalpine scrub, not obvious except in flocks.
— feeds on insects, nectar, berries and fruit.

Breeding:
— August to February, more than one clutch.
— Nest: very flimsy structure of fine grasses and fibres attached like a hammock with spiders' web to twigs or leaves in outermost foliage.
— Eggs: 3–4, clear pale blue, can often be seen through walls of nest.

BELLBIRD ♂

♀

Bellbird
(Korimako, Makomako)

Anthornis melanura
Family: MELIPHAGIDAE

Plate 68

Endemic: Two closely related sub-species. (Fully protected.)

Field Characters:
— size between Song Thrush and House Sparrow.
— tail long with notched end.
— Male: purple gloss on head and face.
— Female: duller, with narrow white stripe on cheek.
— voice often confused with Tui, a liquid flute-like note and a sharp alarm call.

Distribution and Habitat:
— throughout New Zealand, but rarely seen north of Auckland on mainland.
— in larger forest areas, scrub, gardens and orchards.
— feeds on nectar, insects and fruit.
— pollen becomes attached to head when searching for nectar in flax and pohutukawa.

Breeding:
— September to January.
— Nest: loosely constructed of twigs and fibres with a deep cup well lined with feathers and fine grass.
— usually in dense cover up to 12 m.
— Eggs: 3–4, pinkish-white, with reddish-brown spots and blotches densest at larger end.
— female only incubates.

TUI

Tui

Prosthemadera novaeseelandiae
Family: MELIPHAGIDAE

Plate 69

Endemic: One closely related sub-species. (Fully protected.)

Field Characters:
— slightly bigger than Blackbird, male larger.
— prominent white tuft at throat and white patch on wing.
— middle of back dark brown, otherwise black with variable metallic sheen.
— loud whirring of wings especially when taking flight.
— voice similar to Bellbird but more resonant and having harsh croaks and gurgles especially at end of call.

Distribution and Habitat:
— throughout New Zealand up to 1,200 m.
— primarily in native forest remnants, also gardens to which it is attracted by flowering trees and shrubs, rare in pure beech forest.
— feeds on nectar, fruit, berries and insects.
— forehead often pollen-stained.

Breeding:
— October to January, possibly 2 broods.
— Nest: bulky structure of sticks and twigs, cup lined with fine grasses, moss and feathers.
— Eggs: 3–4, pinkish-white with reddish-brown spots and blotches densest at larger end.
— female only incubates.

CIRL BUNTING ♂

♀
YELLOWHAMMER
♂

Yellowhammer

Emberiza citrinella
Family: EMBERIZIDAE

Plate 70

Introduced: From Europe 1860s. (Not protected.)

Field Characters:
— similar in size to House Sparrow.
— Male: bright yellow head and undersides with dark chest band.
— Female: more drab.
— both sexes have conspicuous chestnut rump, and mainly white outer tail feathers which are prominent in flight.
— larger flocks in winter and spring.

Distribution and Habitat:
— throughout New Zealand, mainly in open country up to alpine tussock.
— feeds on seeds and insects.

Breeding:
— October to January, generally 2 broods.
— Nest: generally close to ground in scrub, hedges, fern, gorse, etc., of grasses lined with finer grass and hair.
— Eggs: 3–5, variable pink to purplish-white, erratically patterned with finely pencilled dark lines.

Cirl Bunting

Emberiza cirlus
Family: EMBERIZIDAE

Plate 70

Introduced: From Europe 1870s. (Not protected.)

Field Characters:
— similar to Yellowhammer.
— Male: adult has prominent black throat and eyestripe, olive-green rump.
— Female: no chestnut rump otherwise similar to female Yellowhammer.

Distribution and Habitat:
— mainly east coast of South Island, rare in North Island. Habitat similar to Yellowhammer.

Breeding:
— similar to Yellowhammer, but eggs less prominently marked.

CHAFFINCH ♂

♀

Chaffinch

Fringilla coelebs
Family: FRINGILLIDAE

Plate 71

Introduced: From Europe 1860s. (Not protected.)

Field Characters:
— Male colourful. Female drab. Immature similar to adult female.
— Male and female, have two conspicuous white bars on wing and white outer tail feathers prominent in flight.
— Flight undulating.

Distribution and Habitat:
— throughout New Zealand, nowhere in large numbers.
— mainly gardens, orchards and scrubland, but also throughout exotic forest and native bush up to the scrubline.
— outside the breeding season often in loose flocks of separate sexes.
— during winter, single birds often seen mixed in flocks of other finches.
— feeds on insects, and seeds.

Breeding:
— October to February.
— Nest: neat and tightly woven of moss, grass and fine roots. Always plastered on the outside with moss and lichen, lined with fine grass, thistledown and feathers. Often built close to tree trunk, at fork of branch.
— Eggs: 4–6 *either* purplish and red-brown splodges on a grey to green-blue background *or* pure blue with slight black-purplish spots.

GREENFINCH

♂

♀

Greenfinch
Carduelis chloris
Family: FRINGILLIDAE

Plate 72

Introduced: From Europe 1860s. (Not protected.)

Field Characters:
— larger than House Sparrow.
— forked tail, heavy pale bill.
— Male: olive-green, with bright yellow markings on wings and tail very striking in flight.
— Female and Immature: duller and browner.

Distribution and Habitat:
— quite plentiful throughout New Zealand up to 600 m.
— open country, gardens, hedges and pine plantations.
— flocks in autumn.
— feeds on seeds, fleshy fruits, insect larvae, occasionally leaves and fruit flowers.

Breeding:
— September to January, usually two broods.
— Nest: often in fork rarely higher than 6 m, of fine sticks, roots and moss, lined with feathers, wool and hair.
— Eggs: 4–6, off-white with variable red-brown spots or streaks.
— female only incubates.

GOLDFINCH

Adult

Immature

Goldfinch

Carduelis carduelis
Family: FRINGILLIDAE

Introduced: From Europe 1860s. (Not protected.)

Field Characters:
— smaller than House Sparrow.
— sexes alike.
— distinctive red, white and black head.
— conspicuous broad yellow band on black wings.
— Immature: streaky light brown underside and lacks bright head colours.
— often in flocks.

Distribution and Habitat:
— throughout New Zealand.
— common in settled areas, especially abundant in fruit-growing areas.
— rare above 1,000 m.
— feeds mainly on seed heads, especially composites (dandelion, thistle, etc.) and grasses, insects and their larvae.

Breeding:
— September to December, usually two broods.
— Nest: neat round structure of grass roots, cobwebs, hair, lined either with thistledown, wool or feathers.
— 2–4 m. from ground in trees and shrubs, often in outside branches.
— Eggs: 4–6, bluish-white, with reddish spots and blotches especially at larger end.
— female only incubates.

REDPOLL

♀

♂

Redpoll

Carduelis flammea
Family: FRINGILLIDAE

Plate 74

Introduced: From Europe 1860s. (Not protected.)

Field Characters:
— smaller than House Sparrow and smallest of introduced finches.
— superficially drab.
— Crimson forehead and small black bib.
— the male breast has a variable amount of pink which can sometimes be absent.
— Immature: crimson on forehead absent.

Distribution and Habitat:
— throughout New Zealand, more plentiful in South Island.
— especially in scrubland, generally away from towns, but up to subalpine.
— feeds mainly on seeds, insects and soft parts of plants.

Breeding:
— September to January, often two broods.
— Nest: mainly in shrubs, small and compact of grass, twigs and wool, lined with hair, feathers or wool.
— Eggs: 4–5, bluish-white with dark or light brown spots and streaks.
— female only incubates.

HOUSE SPARROW

♂ Summer

Autumn ♂

♀

House Sparrow

Passer domesticus
Family: **PLOCEIDAE**

Plate 75

Introduced: From Europe 1860s. (Not protected.)

Field Characters:
— most commonly seen bird in built-up areas.
— Males: black bib varying in size, small in autumn, large in summer because of wear of feathers exposing their black bases. Bill black in breeding season, otherwise brown.
— Immature and female: similarly drab.

Distribution and Habitat:
— abundant throughout New Zealand.
— prefers areas close to habitation, less plentiful on open grassland, not penetrating far into forest.
— often in flocks. Large night roosts common in cities.
— feeds widely on insects, seeds, scraps, grain, fruits, flax nectar, according to locality and season.

Breeding:
— July to April, several broods.
— Nest: usually in holes in buildings, trees and cliffs, also colonies in high trees where nests are large untidy-looking structures of grass with side entrances, and lined with feathers.
— Eggs: 5–7, white, generally heavily spotted and streaked with greyish-brown.

STARLING   Adult Winter

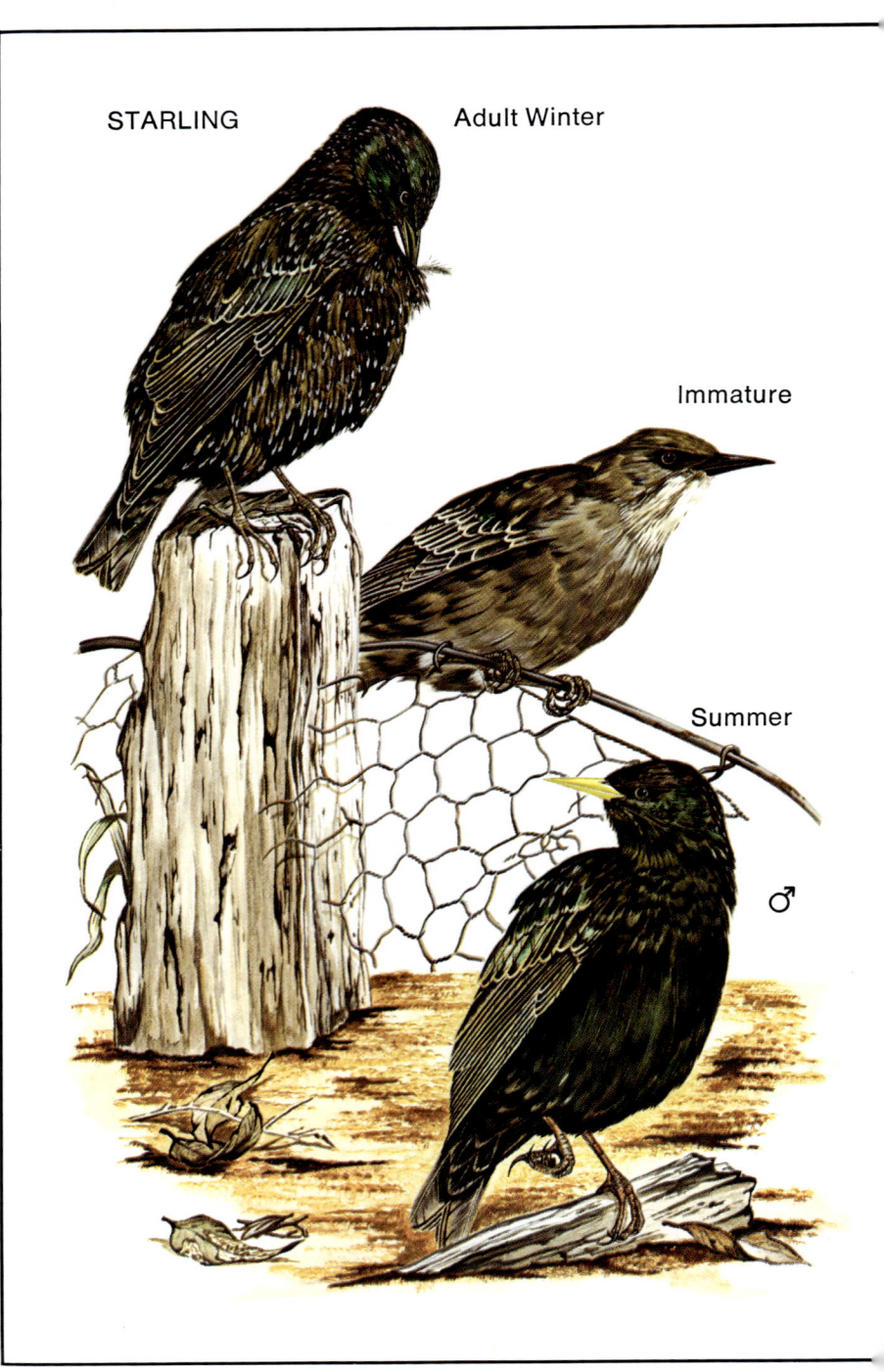

Immature

Summer

♂

Starling

Sturnus vulgaris
Family: STURNIDAE

Plate 76

Introduced: From Europe 1862. (Not protected.)

Field Characters:
— slightly smaller than Blackbird.
— short tail, pointed wings prominent in flight.
— winter plumage: sexes similar, blackish speckled with buff, bill black.
— breeding plumage: bill yellow, males black with purple and green gloss, females retain much of buff speckling.
— Immature: dull brownish buff with dark bill.
— form extensive and noisy roosting flocks outside breeding season.

Distribution and Habitat:
— very common throughout New Zealand, up to subalpine, except in dense bush.
— feeds on worms, insects, fruit, often on open paddocks and beaches.

Breeding:
— September to January, often two broods.
— Nest: in holes in buildings, trees, cliffs and banks, an untidy accumulation of straw and grasses.
— Eggs: 4–6, plain pale blue, with slight gloss.

INDIAN MYNA

Indian Myna

Acridotheres tristis
Family: STURNIDAE

Introduced: Initially from Australia 1870s. (Not protected.)

Field Characters:
— similar in size to Blackbird.
— bright yellow bill, legs and bare patch below eye.
— conspicuous white patch on wing and tip of tail in flight.
— Immature: grey-brown head.
— often form communal night roosts outside breeding season.

Distribution and Habitat:
— plentiful in North Island northwards from Wanganui and Southern Hawke's Bay, occasionally south of this line.
— characteristically in built-up areas, often seen at roadside.
— feeds mainly on insects, some fruit and seeds.

Breeding:
— November to February, generally two broods.
— Nest: an untidy accumulation of grasses, plastics, cellulose and green leaves, in holes in buildings and banks.
— Eggs: 3–5, pale blue.

BLACK-BACKED MAGPIE

♀

♂

Black-backed Magpie   *Gymnorhina tibicen tibicen*
Family: CRACTICIDAE

Plate 78

Introduced: Possibly from Australia, 1860s. (Not protected.)

Field Characters:
— conspicuous black and white bird.
— black back distinguishes this sub-species from White-backed Magpie.
— hindneck white in male but mottled grey in female.
— Immature: mottled grey underside and back, with grey hindneck.
— melodious flute-like call.

Distribution and Habitat:
— Most plentiful in Hawke's Bay and Turakina districts of North Island, Cheviot and Kaikoura in South Island.
— hybridises with White-backed Magpie producing mixed progeny with varying amounts of black on the back. These may be seen over wide areas.
— food as for White-backed Magpie.

Breeding:
— see White-backed Magpie.

WHITE-BACKED MAGPIE

Plate 79

White-backed Magpie *Gymnorhina tibicen hypoleuca*
Family: CRACTICIDAE

Introduced: From Australia 1860s. (Not protected.)

Field Characters:
— similar to Black-backed Magpie.
— Male: back white.
— Female: back grey.
— Immature: similar to female but with mottled grey underside.
— melodious flute-like call.

Distribution and Habitat:
— throughout New Zealand except thick bush and alpine areas.
— commonly on outskirts of built-up areas including parks, golf courses, etc.
— feeds generally on insects, worms, occasionally eggs and young of ground-nesting birds.

Breeding:
— August to November, occasionally two broods.
— Nest: usually in tall trees, an untidy collection of twigs, wire and other sundries often used, lined with roots and fibres.
— Eggs: 2–5, bluish-green, heavily blotched all over with greyish-brown.

Note:
Boldly defends its nesting territory by dive-bombing intruders, including human beings who approach the area too closely.

ROOK   Adult

Immature

Rook

Corvus frugilegus
Family: CORVIDAE

Plate 80

Introduced: From Europe 1860s. (Not protected.)

Field Characters:
— bigger than Magpie.
— all black with bluish gloss and large black bill, sexes alike.
— only adults have bare grey skin surrounding base of bill.
— deliberate wing beat.
— large flocks form regular night roosts outside breeding season.

Distribution and Habitat:
— mainly Hawke's Bay, South Wairarapa and Canterbury, with largest concentration in Hawke's Bay. Occasional elsewhere.
— open country and plantations.
— feeds on insects, worms, larvae, seeds and vegetable matter.

Breeding:
— September to October.
— Nest: in tops of large trees, large and untidy of twigs and mud with grass lining, used from year to year.
— generally close together forming "rookeries" which may be very large.
— Eggs: 2–4, pale bluish-green closely covered with greyish brown blotches and spots.

Index of Common Names

	Page	Plate
Bellbird	139	68
Bittern	29	13
Blackbird	135	66
Bunting, Cirl	143	70
Chaffinch	145	71
Creeper, Brown	119	58
Coot	61	29
Cuckoo, Long-tailed	99	48
Cuckoo, Shining	99	48
Dabchick	11	4
Dotterel, Banded	67	32
Dotterel, Black-fronted	69	33
Duck, Blue	45	21
Duck, Grey	39	18
Falcon (NZ)	49	23
Fantail	127	62
Fernbird	117	57
Gannet	13	5
Godwit, E. Bar-tailed	73	35
Goldfinch	149	73
Goose, Canada	33	15
Greenfinch	147	72
Gull, Black-backed	77	37
Gull, Black-billed	81	39
Gull, Red-billed	79	38
Harrier	47	22
Heron, Reef	27	12
Heron, White	25	11
Heron, White-faced	23	10
Kaka	93	45
Kea	93	45
Kingfisher	105	51
Kiwi	5	1
Magpie, Black-backed	159	78
Magpie, White-backed	161	79
Mallard	37	17
Morepork	101	49
Myna	157	77
Owl, Little	103	50
Oystercatcher, South Island Pied	63	30
Oystercatcher, Variable	63	30
Parakeet, Red-crowned	97	47
Parakeet, Yellow-crowned	97	47
Penguin, Blue	9	3
Penguin, Fiordland Crested	7	2
Penguin, White-flippered	9	3
Penguin, Yellow-eyed	7	2
Pheasant	53	25
Pigeon, New Zealand	89	43
Pigeon, Rock	91	44
Pipit	111	54
Plover, Spur-winged	65	31
Pukeko	59	28

	Page	Plate
Quail, California	51	24
Rail, Banded	55	26
Redpoll	151	74
Rifleman	107	52
Robin	131	64
Rook	163	80
Rosella, Eastern	95	46
Scaup	41	19
Shag, Black	15	6
Shag, Little	17	7
Shag, Little Black	17	7
Shag, Pied	15	6
Shag, Spotted	21	9
Shag, Stewart Island	19	8
Shelduck, Paradise	35	16
Shoveler	43	20
Silvereye	137	67
Skylark	111	54
Sparrow, Hedge	115	56
Sparrow, House	153	75
Spoonbill, Royal	25	11
Starling	155	76
Stilt, Pied	75	36
Swallow, Welcome	113	55
Swan, Black	31	14
Teal, Grey	41	19
Tern, Black-fronted	83	40
Tern, Caspian	85	41
Tern, White-fronted	87	42
Thrush, Song	133	65
Tit	129	63
Tui	141	69
Warbler, Grey	125	61
Weka	57	27
Whitehead	121	59
Wren, Rock	109	53
Wrybill	71	34
Yellowhammer	143	70
Yellowhead	123	60

- Girl Bunting
- Australasian Harrier
- Yellowhead
- Yellow Hammer
- Gold Finch
- Song Thrush
- Blackbird
- NZ Pidgeon
- Kingfisher
- Chaffinch
- Fantail
- Canada Goose
- Greenfinch
- Gull Black Backed
- White Faced Heron
- Magpie White Backed
- Mallard
- Myna
- Pheasant
- Plover Spur Winged
- Oyster Catcher
- Pukeko
- Pidgeon Rock
- Quail Californian
- Rosella Eastern
- Shag Black
- Shag Little Black
- Paradise Shellduck
- Swallow Welcome
- Swan Black
- Tui
- Tern White Fronted
- Starling
- Sparrow House
- Skylark
- Mallard
- Grey Duck
- Bell Bird
- Grey Warbler
- Silver Eye
- NZ Scaup
- Black Billed Gull
- Shag Pied
- Tern Caspian
- Red Billed Gull
- Banded Dotterel
- Sooty Shearwater
- Weka
- Cockatoo Sulphur Crested
- Shining Cuckoo 5
- Hedge Sparrow
- NZ Pippit
- (Eastern Bartailed Godwit)
- Australasian Coot
- Cuckoo Long Tailed 5x
- Gannet
- White Heron
- Wild Turkey
- Magpie Black Backed
- Pied Stilt